Yorkshire
Wisdom

*A selection of quotes from the famous and
the not so famous of God's Own County*

By Joe Moorwood

Illustrated by Rowan Moorwood

GREAT NORTHERN

For Iris

Great Northern Books
PO Box 213, Ilkley, LS29 9WS
www.greatnorthernbooks.co.uk

Every effort has been made to acknowledge correctly
and contact the copyright holders of material in this
book. Great Northern Books apologises for any
unintentional errors or omissions, which should be
notified to the publisher.

ISBN: 978-0-9928193-8-5

Design and layout: David Burrill

CIP Data
A catalogue for this book is available
from the British Library

Contents

#YorkshireWisdom

Introduction

The book you hold in your hand contains a collection of advice and observations from some of Yorkshire's most celebrated sons and daughters – of which there are many! There is, however, a slight twist. Being a Yorkshire-born book, it only felt natural to keep things grounded and not lose ourselves entirely in the words of celebrities.

Every day, quote-worthy statements are composed that don't get much further than a family circle, a group of friends or even the minds of their creators. With this in mind, I made it my mission to unearth some genuine pearls of wisdom from 'ordinary' Yorkshire folk across the county.

These cranial treasures have been extracted from friends and family, colleagues, neighbours, and often complete strangers (you can read more about this fascinating process later in the book). Their quotations now rightly share the stage, or rather the page, with the words of those already guaranteed a place in Yorkshire folklore.

From the insightful to the amusing and from the inspiring to the downright obscure, the good people of Yorkshire are rarely short of an opinion.

Life is a lesson

If you would have your son to walk honorably through the world, you must not attempt to clear the stones from his path, but teach him to walk firmly over them – not insist on leading him by the hand, but let him learn to go alone.

Anne Bronte, novelist and poet, from West Yorkshire

One of the biggest mistakes you can make is to always avoid situations where you might make a mistake.

Bryan, teacher, from Leeds

If I could go back in time and talk to my younger self, I wouldn't get bogged down in any of that learn from your mistakes, no regrets nonsense. I'd provide myself with a blow-by-blow account of where, when and how I've screwed up.

Ian, plumber, from Sheffield

Never mix cider and red wine. That's one of my life lessons.

Jarvis Cocker, musician and front man, from Sheffield

The most important thing about self-reflection is getting the balance right. Too much, and you'll become a neurotic mess. Too little and you're probably a bit of a dick.

Paul, IT consultant, from North Yorkshire

Opening your mind involves more than listening to progressive music, smoking the occasional spliff and watching a foreign film. Accepting how brainwashed we all are, is a good start.

Jane, designer, from Beverley

If in doubt don't react, observe.

Elaine, dinner lady, from Rotherham

What I have known with respect to myself has tended much to lessen both my admiration, and my contempt, of others.

Joseph Priestley, 18th century theologian and writer, from West Yorkshire

Carl: *It's times like this that I really wish I'd listened to what my dad once said to me when I was a lad.*
Ryan: *What did he say?*
Carl: *I don't know, I wasn't listening.*

Carl, web designer, from Halifax

Allowing others to laugh at your misfortune and taking pleasure from their laughter is a great way to recycle bad luck into something good.

Janine, from Ripon (Twitter)

If something bad happens in your life the chances are, you created it, promoted it or at the very least allowed it to happen. If none of those apply then you're in to the realms of luck - but if you're truly honest, this is rarely the case. You should remember though that this applies to the good stuff too. Learn to take some credit now and then.

Todd, software engineer, from Wath upon Dearne

I don't think that making ourselves invulnerable to feeling any onslaught to our feelings will help us in life, ultimately. I think we only learn and grow by allowing ourselves to be really challenged by those feelings that do overwhelm us occasionally.

Sir Ben Kingsley, actor, from North Yorskhire

Most of the important lessons I learnt at school were in the playground.

Freddy, student, from Bradford

The majority of students taking night classes all share the same regret – why the hell didn't I appreciate the opportunity to learn when I was at school?

Gabriella, teacher, from Sheffield

Our inability to accept what is out of our hands is a childhood trait we all struggle to shake entirely. But, I can tell you, it's worth shaking.

Gary, retired police officer, from Leeds

Since I've had cancer I've realised that every day is a bonus.

Sir Geoffrey Boycott, cricketer, from West Yorkshire

They don't test your judgment of character in any school exam I ever took, but I'm pretty sure that's more useful than Latin or algebra.

Sally, veterinary technician, from North Yorkshire

Someone once asked me if you had to remove 10% of the world's population, where would you start. A dark, disturbing and weird question - but have a serious think about it and you'll find out a bit about yourself!

Bob, database administrator, from Wakefield (Twitter)

One of the most important human rights should be the right to make mistakes… occasionally.

Ankita, marketing officer, from West Yorkshire

When a thing's done it's done. And if it's not done right, do it differently next time.

Arthur Ransome, author and journalist, from Leeds

If you could somehow bottle hindsight and sell it to people in advance, you'd be rich.

Arthur, retired steelworker, from Sheffield

I often look back at myself and see a different person to the man I am today. But I don't think you should ever attempt to fully detach yourself from any of your past lives. I don't believe in the mantra 'no regrets'. Just learn to love yourself in the past and the present. Whatever you did and whoever you were, you had your reasons.

Unknown, from Yorkshire (Twitter)

Don't ask who's to blame or how can I hide this, but what can I learn from this?

Pete, from East Yorkshire

The secret of life is to have a task, something you devote your entire life to. Something you bring everything to, every minute of the day for the rest of your life. And the most important thing is, it must be something you cannot possibly do.

Henry Moore, sculptor and artist, from West Yorkshire

Know it all's should know that if indeed they do know it all, there's no need for everyone else to know they know it all.

Rob, community nurse, from Doncaster

Pettiness, jealousy, vindictiveness, and other childlike qualities are usually easier to spot in other people than ourselves.

Henry, mental health analyst, from Sheffield

Honest criticism is bloody hard to take, and the truer it is the more it smarts.

Vern, unemployed, from Leeds

There is always a 'but' in this imperfect world.

Anne Bronte, novelist and poet from West Yorkshire

So many words of wisdom are based on overcoming adversity - the school of hard-knocks, every challenge is an opportunity… all that stuff. There's plenty to be learnt from nice things and good fortune, it just doesn't carry quite the same punch as the tough stuff.

June, housewife, from Sheffield

I've always tried to create an illusion of knowing less than I actually do. I've met a lot of people who try the opposite of that and I rarely like them very much.

John, sales rep, from Sheffield

I think in terms of the day's resolutions, not the year's.

Henry Moore, sculptor and artist, from West Yorkshire

Ryan: *Do you ever wonder what would happen if you just walked away and left it all behind?*

Sarah: *You'd search and search, until that glorious day when you found something else to run away from.*

Husband and wife, from North Yorkshire

I'll walk where my own nature would be leading: It vexes me to choose another guide.

Emily Bronte, novelist and poet from West Yorkshire

Teacher: *Stop day dreaming, pay attention and listen to me! What is going on in that head of yours?*

Naughty boy: *Summit' more interesting than thee.*

From a secondary school in Sheffield

Cradle to the
care home

To show a child what has once delighted you, to find the child's delight added to your own, so that there is now a double delight seen in the glow of trust and affection, this is happiness.

John Boynton Priestley, writer and broadcaster, from Bradford

Telling a sulking three year old that they can play again tomorrow is like telling a grown-up football fan that England might do better at the next world cup.

Shane, househusband, from South Yorkshire

Me: *Can you count to ten?*

Noah *(my three year old son): Yes daddy… one, two, three, four, five, six, seven, eight, nine, ten!*

Me: *Can you count backwards?*

Noah: *(thinks)… Yep. (turns his back on me) one, two, three, four…*

An exchange somewhere in Sheffield

Every single person is vulnerable to unexpected defeat in this inmost emotional self. At every moment, behind the most efficient seeming adult exterior, the whole world of the person's childhood is being carefully held like a glass of water bulging above the brim. And in fact, that child is the only real thing in them. It's their humanity, their real individuality, the one that can't understand why it was born and that knows it will have to die, in no matter how crowded a place, quite on its own. That's the carrier of all the living qualities. It's the centre of all the possible magic and revelation.

Ted Hughes, writer and poet, from West Yorkshire

There is no more heart-warming a sound than that of a fully committed and uncontrollable belly laugh from your toddler, especially if you are the comedian responsible for it.

Joe, from Thirsk

Encourage your children to do whatever makes them happy, not what you think should make them happy.

Jasmine, sales assistant, from Scarborough (Twitter)

Sometimes I see a kid being sworn and shouted at in the supermarket, and I wonder, what are the chances they won't be doing the same to their kids in the future?

Tim, firefighter, from South Yorkshire

As we read the school reports on our children, we realise a sense of relief that can rise to delight, that thank Heaven no one is reporting in this fashion on us.

Joseph Priestley, 18th century theologian and writer, from West Yorkshire

Enthusiasm and imagination can get overly diluted with drive and discipline if you're pushed too hard at school. A child's limitless imagination should be protected and nurtured.

Kim, from Yorkshire (Twitter)

One of the nice things about teenagers is that they don't know it's all been done before.

George, between jobs, from Sheffield

Youth would be an ideal state if it came a little later in life

Herbert Henry Asquith, Prime Minister, from West Yorkshire

It's a frustrating fact that the young don't appreciate being young until they're old enough to tell younger people how much they should appreciate being young.

Thomas, from Yorkshire (Twitter)

Like its politicians and its wars, society has the teenagers it deserves.

John Boynton Priestley, writer and broadcaster, from Bradford

I still look around for someone else when a child points at me and refers to me as a man. I'm 23.

Jamie, student, from Leeds

I don't think you're a proper grown-up until you become a parent.

Marie, PR consultant, from Wakefield

The best thing about being a mum is caring about another human more than yourself - especially if you were previously a self-absorbed narcissist like I was.

Carla, from Hull (Twitter)

It's only family and very close friends that are really that interested in our lives. Actually, I'll refine that further… It's only our mums that are truly interested in our lives.

Jeremy, postman, from Barnsley

A man leaned over to a man in a pub
And said in a voice
'I used to be thirty seven but now I'm fifty one'.
And that's how the years go.
In handfuls.
Like somebody is almost at the end of a bag of
crisps
And they tip the bag up
And it's as though they're drinking crisps.
That's how the years go.

Ian McMillan, poet, writer and broadcaster, from South Yorkshire

If you've not grown up by the time you're 40, you may as we'll not bother.

Ho, barman, from York

I've got to an age where I just can't be arsed doing things that make me feel crap.

Jarvis Cocker, musician and front man, from Sheffield

When you are under 50 you want to look good and when you are over 50 you want to feel good. Then when you feel good, you look good.

KiKi Dee, singer, from West Yorkshire

It's better to burn out, than to fade away.

Def Leppard, rock band, from Sheffield

Inspiration, moral guidance, and all that...

Let everyone regulate his conflict… by the golden rule of doing to others as in similar circumstances we would have them do to us, and the path of duty will be clear before him.

William Wilberforce, politician and philanthropist (leader of the movement to abolish the slave trade), from Kingston upon Hull

Change the things that can be changed, accept those that cannot, and have the wisdom to know when it's time to go to the pub.

Des, events planner, from Leeds

And that's how we measure out our real respect for people—by the degree of feeling they can register, the voltage of life they can carry and tolerate—and enjoy.

Ted Hughes, writer and poet, from West Yorkshire

Do, learn and enjoy. There's not much more to say.

Joseph, retired prison guard, from South Yorkshire

Listen to people and treat them as you find them. There's an inherent goodness in most people. Don't pre-judge people – that was me Mam's advice anyway.

Sean Bean, actor, from Sheffield

You can force yourself to be kind but you can't make yourself like someone.

Janet, landlady, from North Yorkshire

If we can only speak to slander our betters, let us hold our tongues

Anne Bronte, novelist and poet, from West Yorkshire

Me mam always said if you've got nout good to say, don't say out.

Kelly, from Huddersfield (Twitter)

Honesty will scare most people off, but it will attract the right ones.

Mr Sood, from Yorkshire

Back in the day a promise was a promise. These days there's a shallowness to things. Maybe I'm being old fashioned but a bloke's word used to mean something when I were a youth.

A man in a Sheffield pub

I would always rather be happy than dignified.

Charlotte Bronte, novelist and poet, from West Yorkshire

My dad was a happy man. He always said that love and curiosity were enough for him.

Holly, student, from Ripley (Twitter)

Boredom can be a big inspiration, because you have to invent something to entertain yourself, otherwise you go crackers.

Jarvis Cocker, musician and front man, from Sheffield

Everybody should have a party trick of some kind. It doesn't have to be much, but they should have one nonetheless.

Sid, barman, from West Yorkshire

You sometimes hear people say that happiness is all about appreciating the little things. I think that belittles the so-called little things.

Jules, from Beverley

Even in this modern world, with all its technology and advancements, a sick person is an unhappy person. It's a cliché, but you have to appreciate good health when its there, because when it's gone it's the only thing that matters.

Ian, roofer, from Huddersfield

If you can't help yourself, help someone else.

Rowan, retired dentist, from Sheffield

Remember to care for the soul more than the body...

Saint Alcuin of York (8th century)

If you want to feel better about yourself, just do good things and remember that you did them. It's not rocket science.

Man in a pub, in Leeds

We're all approval seekers. That's not necessarily a bad thing, just as long as we're seeking the right kind of approval from the right kind of people.

Ali, taxi driver, from Harrogate

Dishonesty is fundamentally wrong. But it is the motivation behind a lie that determines how wrong it is.

Lauren, careers adviser, from West Yorkshire (Twitter)

It's easy to forget that there's a choice in how we perceive things and how we react to situations. Habitual and instinctive responses lead to so much day-to-day misery.

Ben, from Yorkshire

Any action that makes you lose self-respect is a wrong action.

Anon, from Yorkshire (Twitter)

You may choose to look the other way but you can never say again that you did not know.

William Wilberforce, politician, philanthropist and leader of the movement to abolish the slave trade, from Kingston upon Hull

Accepting your innate selfish streak is liberating, and entirely necessary if you want to find the good stuff that lies beneath.

Mick, writer, from Wetherby (Twitter)

We must love friends for their sake rather than our own.

Charlotte Bronte, novelist and poet, from West Yorkshire

If you wrote everyone off for being hypocritical, you'd soon run out of friends.

Keith, psychologist, from Guiseley

The more pleasure you can take from other people's good qualities, the more likely you are to possess these qualities in yourself.

Rene, from Yorkshire (Twitter)

Promise me you will always remember that you are braver than you believe, stronger than you seem, and smarter than you think.

Corrine Bailey Rae, singer, from Leeds

If you could see what the people you dislike have been exposed to, you'd probably be more forgiving. The people I admire most are those who can break generational cycles and become better people than those around them.

Joshua, lecturer, from Leeds

Some people are turned on by what divides, and some get their kicks from what unites us. I recommend the latter of these people.

Anon, from Yorkshire (Twitter)

If to be feelingly alive to the sufferings of my fellow creatures is to be a fanatic, I am one of the most incurable fanatics ever to be at large.

William Wilberforce, politician and philanthropist (leader of the movement to abolish the slave trade), from Kingston upon Hull

If your actions don't mirror your beliefs you have to change your actions or change your beliefs. Unhappiness waits if not.

Jamil, pharmacist, from Halifax (Twitter)

War and conflict are unfortunately infused in human nature as much as love and understanding. It's going to take a significant leap in evolution to change this fact. In the meantime I suggest you appreciate the love and understanding bit.

Joshua, lecturer, from Leeds

I think, what has this day brought me, and what have I given it?

Henry Moore, sculptor and artist, from West Yorkshire

Appreciating the little things is the opposite of blowing small things out of proportion. They both carry the same logic (or lack of) it's just that one makes us feel good, and the other bad. So it's just commonsense really.

Anna, housewife, from Sheffield

'The truth' and 'the now' are all there really is - yet both are hard to hold on to, hard to define. If you can capture either of them you'll do alright.

Toby, bar owner, from Harrogate

Science, philosophy, and other clever stuff…

Genetics...

William Bateson, the first geneticist to use the term genetics, from North Yorkshire

I am well convinced that 'Aerial Navigation' will form a most prominent feature in the progress of civilisation.

Sir George Cayley, built the first successful man carrying glider, from Scarborough

Things are the way they are, because they were the way they were.

Sir Fred Hoyle, astronomer, from West Yorkshire

It's amazing how lonely and disconnected from the world people can feel. We owe every single thought in our heads to everything that ever has been and ever will be.

Esther, from South Yorkshire

Here we are,
Lent to the earth by the stars

Richard Hawley, singer and musician, from Sheffield

People sometimes say you can't live in the past and you shouldn't live for the future. It's an obvious and perfectly reasonable sentiment, but you can't consciously capture time and deliberately try to live in the moment. If you're aware of this concept we call the now, you'll not be able to genuinely experience it, you'll not be able to cut it… 'Cutting the now'… I like that.

Rowan, retired Dentist, from Sheffield

To know one thing, you must know the opposite.

Henry Moore, sculptor and artist, from West Yorkshire

Joe: Philosophy is to science what Latin is to languages.

John: Mathematics is to science what Latin is to languages.

Conversation in a Sheffield cafe

If a man speaks in a forest and there is no woman there to hear… is he still wrong?

Chris, firefighter, from Barnsley (Twitter)

What came first, the chicken or the dickhead?

Alex Turner, musician and front man, from Sheffield

Dave (after several pints) attempting to tell a science-based joke: *If a physicist is an atom's way about knowing about atoms, then a drunk is beer's way about knowing about… No, wait, if a drunk physicist knows about atoms then that's… no, seriously, hang on. If an atom is a physasiph… pyhysa… physicist's way about atoms…*

Dave's wife Pauline: *Do you know, I once read that we think on average well over a thousand words per minute? Hard to believe, isn't it.*

From a pub in Leeds

It is seldom at the frontier that discoveries are made but more often in the dustbin.

Alan Bennett, playwright, screenwriter, actor and author, from West Yorkshire

There aren't really any new things to discover in life. The same things have obsessed people throughout the centuries. We're not going to invent a new colour now. So this is all there is. Everything else is your imagination. So use it well.

Jarvis Cocker, musician and front man, from Sheffield

The modern world has screwed up natural selection for humans. The slower, dim-witted types that might have been killed off by a saber-toothed tiger back in the day; they're now the ones that have more kids than anyone else.

Matt, engineer, from Rotherham

Self-preservation, nature's first great law, all the creatures, except man, doth awe

Andrew Marvell, 17th century metaphysical poet and politician, from East Yorkshire

The fight-or-flight-reflex Mother Nature so kindly provided us with feels sickeningly misplaced in many modern day scenarios. Sprinting out the room or attacking the nearest person isn't going to do you much good in an exam, job interview, or best man's speech...

Mr Drake, from Towthorpe (Twitter)

*From an evolutionary point of view we're
programmed to look for danger, for what's wrong.
I think that's why there's a lot of internal confusion
out there. Maybe things are too safe for some
people to cope.*

Matt, engineer, from Rotherham

*We're all driven by animal instincts dressed up as
summit' else.*

Ray, plasterer, from West Yorkshire

**We must beware the revenge of the starved senses,
the embittered animal in its prison.**

**John Boynton Priestley, writer and broadcaster, from
Bradford**

There's a hum of muted sex and muffled violence.

Amy, civil servant, from Sheffield – describing the atmosphere
at work, after the introduction of a new open-plan office layout

Unfortunately, morality has not evolved at the same pace as other human advancements. We've leaped from looking after a small inner circle and ourselves, to national and global responsibility in a relatively short period of time. It's all very confusing being a human.

Joseph, firefighter, from Sheffield

In our brief time here, what we perceive of this thing we call life is so very limited, from the point of view of our five basic senses. However, I believe that the whole is greater than the sum of its parts when it comes to the human mind. It's that little bit extra that makes us all so special.

Hannah, psychiatrist, from East Yorkshire (Twitter)

A master of words can sculpt reality, for good or for evil.

Anon, from Yorkshire, Twitter

The more elaborate our means of communication, the less we communicate.

Joseph Priestley, 18th century theologian and writer, from West Yorkshire

Last Wednesday I stupidly dropped my iPhone in the bath and my life has sort of spiralled almost out of control.

Patrick Stewart, actor, from West Yorkshire

Everyone's addicted to iPhones. It's not right. It freaks me out. I hear mine beep and try to ignore it. But the compulsion to get it out of my pocket and check it is unhealthily strong. And 99 times out of 100, whatever it is can wait.

Bob, IT technician, from Hebden Bridge

And one thing's for certain: the net is here forever,
Constant as taxes, as unpredictable as the weather…

And before I'm dragged right under in a growing tide of spam
I've time for just this one last post: I click therefore I am!

(Extract from 'Connected')

Ian McMillan, poet, writer and broadcaster, from South Yorkshire

Highs and lows

Fortune, how fickle and how vain thou art.

Branwell Bronte, painter, writer and poet, from West Yorkshire

The pleasure gained from something bad ending is often worth the something bad occurring.

Mr Moorsgrove, from Yorkshire (Twitter)

I am an optimist, but an optimist who carries a raincoat.

Harold Wilson, Prime Minister, from Huddersfield

Life isn't fair. I realised that the first time I went to Bramall Lane.

Jim, estate agent, from Sheffield

I'm only human
Of flesh and blood I'm made
Human
Born to make mistakes

The Human League, pop band, from Sheffield

I mistrust total competence. I've always felt life is a series of small disasters we try to get through.

Michael Palin, comedian, actor, writer and presenter, from Sheffield

And without warning his face became wet
He thought that he'd learned how to not get upset

Alex Turner, musician and front man, from Sheffield

That's the paradox: the only time most people feel alive is when they're suffering, when something overwhelms their ordinary, careful armour, and the naked child is flung out onto the world. That's why the things that are worst to undergo are best to remember. But when that child gets buried away under their adaptive and protective shells—he becomes one of the walking dead, a monster.

Ted Hughes, writer and poet, from West Yorkshire

And though I tried so not to suffer the indignity of reaction
There were no cracks to grasp or gaps to claw

The Arctic Monkeys (Alex Turner), rock n roll band, from Sheffield

I can tell you from experience that the words 'life goes on' can be the last thing you want to hear in your darkest hour.

Man in a pub, North Yorkshire

The shadows are as important as the light.

Charlotte Bronte, novelist and poet, from West Yorkshire

The majority of people perform well in a crisis and when the spotlight is on them; it's on the Sunday afternoons of this life, when nobody is looking, that the spirit falters.

Alan Bennett, playwright, screenwriter, actor and author, from West Yorkshire

Is there anything sadder than an unshared sorrow?

Anon, from Yorkshire (Twitter)

Until you've had depression I don't think you're qualified to talk about it.

Sir Geoffrey Boycott, cricketer, from West Yorkshire

Once you start peeling the psychological onion and digging beneath your outer layers, you have to keep going until you reach something real. Otherwise you can get lost in no-mans-land.

Kate, doctor, from Sheffield

Cheerfulness, it would appear, is a matter which depends fully as much on the state of things within, as on the state of things without and around us.

Charlotte Bronte, novelist and poet, from West Yorkshire

Aye, it's a funny thing yer 'ead.

Dave, from Guiseley

I note at the age of ten a fully developed ability not quite to enjoy myself, a capacity I have retained intact ever since.

Alan Bennett, playwright, screenwriter, actor and author, from West Yorkshire

Snuffing out anger before it rises to the surface is a skill worth acquiring. You have to sense it almost immediately; before it builds, from a little twinge in your chest to something much more destructive that takes over your whole being. That little twinge doesn't hang around for long waiting for you to make your mind up.

Steve, ex football hooligan, from Sheffield

Is it just me, or is everything shit?

Ricky Wilson, singer, front man and pop panel judge, from West Yorkshire

He's one of those blokes who's thankful for something to whine and moan about, because he'd have bugger all to say if things were always fine and dandy.

Louise, nurse, from Hebden Bridge

A good night's sleep is essential to get a break from the person who drives you up the wall more than anyone else – yourself.

Cameron, between jobs, from Leeds

To tell the truth I honestly don't like myself. I bore the crap out of myself, I really do.

Jarvis Cocker, musician and front man, from Sheffield

I have always been delighted at the prospect of a new day, a fresh try, one more start, with perhaps a bit of magic waiting somewhere behind the morning.

John Boynton Priestley, writer and broadcaster, from Bradford

I heard someone say that a new day is perfect when it arrives. It doesn't usually take long for me to change that. In fact it's usually pretty much gone to shit some time after mid-morning.

Jon, from Castleford

The best things in life can't be controlled, quantified, organized, arranged, computed or dissected. They can't be systemized, calculated or regulated. It's the real and raw stuff that I turn to when nothing else makes sense. The stuff that's been there since before humans learnt to read and write.

Miss Chapman, from Yorkshire (Twitter)

Learn to let go. That's what me mam always tried to instil in me after watching me nearly destroy me-sen wi' booze and other stuff. Took me a long time to understand what she were on about. I know now though. I bloody know now. Learn to let go pal, put that in yer book.

Man in the pub, Sheffield

I'm drunk on truth.

The Cult, indie rock band, from Bradford

Drink to enhance a good time, not to diminish a bad time.

Emma, mature student, from Sheffield

And she won't be surprised, and she won't be shocked
When she's pressed the star after she's pressed unlock
And there's verse and chapter sat in her inbox
And all that it says is that you've drank a lot

The Arctic Monkeys (Alex Turner), rock n roll band, from Sheffield

Anyone who's ever overcome a serious addiction carries with them an inner strength and self-knowledge that can't be obtained in any other way.

Owen, cashier, from Bridlington

Resentment and guilt are essentially the same things. One is directed at others and the other one is directed at yourself. It's best not to harbour either of them if you can help it.

Delia, retired admin officer, from Horbury

Death, religion and
that kind of thing…

Only two things are certain in life. Death, and the outcome of an England match when it goes to penalties.

Matt, events manager, from York

The complete sense of silence and separation when you lose a loved one is something you simply cannot prepare for. But love's joy and pain go hand in hand. And in the end, it is always worth it.

Amelia, from Yorkshire (Twitter)

But say what you will, 'tis better to be left than never to have been loved. To pass our youth in dull indifference, to refuse the sweets of life because they once must leave us, is as preposterous as to wish to have been born old, because we one day must be old.

William Congreve, 15th/16th century playwright and poet, from West Yorkshire

I saw an old friend in a dream last night. It's the only place we meet now. But it's real to me. He told me I was dreaming. I said I know, it doesn't matter, you're here right now. Then I woke up. I'll see him again soon enough.

Anon, from Sheffield

We only live once. For the very lucky and the very unlucky this is probably enough.

Mike, architect, from Hull

Sex and death are the most fundamentally significant aspects of our existence, yet openly talking about either subject is usually considered to be in bad taste.

Nicola, housewife, from South Yorkshire

Grandma, you're so lucky because you're so very old but you're not dead yet.

Joe, age 7, from Sheffield

When you've been that close to dying, you re-evaluate what's really important to you - and it's nothing to do with fame and money.

Chris Rea, singer and musician, from North Yorkshire

They say live everyday as if it were your last? You'd be in a permanent state of panic!

Felix, artist, from Harrogate

You don't have to be friends with death, but it's probably best to be on speaking terms before it arrives.

Lesley, retired teacher, from West Yorkshire

She didn't worry about dying, she saw it as her next journey.

Mike Tomlinson, husband to inspirational fundraiser Jane Tomlinson, West Yorkshire

Don't send me flowers when I'm dead. If you like me, send them while I'm alive

Brian Clough, football manager and player, from North Yorkshire

There's no better way of forgetting something than by commemorating it.

Alan Bennett, playwright, screenwriter, actor and author, from West Yorkshire

If you're spending too much time worrying about death, it's probably a sign that everything else in your life is going pretty well.

Liam, electrician, from Goldthorpe

I would like to believe in the afterlife; it makes things more palatable. But I'm not banking on it.

Jarvis Cocker, musician and front man, from Sheffield

There is a coherent plan to the universe, though I don't know what it's a plan for.

Sir Fred Hoyle, astronomer, from West Yorkshire

Whatever one's religious stance the story of Jesus still resonates. If it did happen – wow. If it didn't, then it's a credit to the genius of humankind for coming up with such a timelessly relevant story.

Rachel, full-time mum, from Sheffield

I'm not even religious. But when someone appears onstage and wants to be Jesus, I think it's a bit off.

Jarvis Cocker, musician and front man, from Sheffield

Most religions were created from the same moral blueprint. That blueprint exists within all of us regardless of our cultural inheritance.

Mohamed, student, from Bradford (Twitter)

We don't live alone. We are members of one body. We are responsible for each other. And I tell you that the time will soon come when if men will not learn that lesson, then they will be taught it in fire and blood and anguish. Good night.

John Boynton Priestley, writer and broadcaster, from Bradford

**Don't let the b*stards
grind you down**

Fear of failure is instilled in us from a very early age in western society. It's heart-breaking to recognise it in a child's eyes, knowing how deep that fear can penetrate if we're not vigilant.

Mr Hughes, from Allerthorpe (Twitter)

Follow your dream. There's no one like you, we've all got something that no one else has got. Follow your dream and don't let the bastards grind you down.

Brian Blessed, actor, from South Yorkshire

I believe we all have a journey. I was once a small girl from Sheffield, dealing with bullies, and normal teenage insecurities, but I always believed. And when you do that, life can get unbelievable.

Jessica Ennis, track and field Olympic champion, from Sheffield

Life is one contradiction after another, and if you can't find the humour in that then you're going to struggle.

Luke, sales rep, from Bramhope

Tragedy need not be a downer.

Sir Ben Kingsley, actor, from North Yorskhire

All great and honourable actions are accompanied with great difficulties, and both must be enterprised and overcome with answerable courage.

William Bradford, 15th century Plymouth Governor and pilgrim father, from South Yorkshire

Laughter is the last line of defence. If that breaks, you're really in trouble mate.

Leon, Taxi driver, from South Yorkshire

Are we going to fight the Germans, or f*** them?

Stanley Hollis, VC winning soldier, from North Yorkshire. After being handed condoms moments before storming the beaches at Normandy

What anybody else thinks about you is really of no consequence. It's what you think of yourself.

David Coverdale, rock singer, from North Yorkshire

Saying nothing at the right time can give you more control of a confrontational situation than anything else.

Elaine, dinner lady, from Rotherham

Where's everyone's patience gone these days? Jesus, can't people just get along, wait their turn and have a bit of patience? And will somebody please get me a f'cking drink?!

Man in a Leeds pub, after breaking up an argument at the bar

They say you should imagine your enemies as old people and it makes them less intimidating. I prefer to imagine them at their funerals.

Janet, landlady, from North Yorkshire

I find I get a better reaction from people once I am less bothered about their reaction.

William Hague, politician, from Rotherham

I spent way too long in my life trying to prove my worthiness, to my friends, my family, people at work. And in hindsight, it was because I didn't feel worthy in myself. Now that's changed I don't try so hard. And I may be wrong, but I'm pretty sure people prefer me now.

Christine, from Shipley (Twitter)

I may be blind, but I can see how inspiring it is to be me.

David Blunkett, politician, from Sheffield

If I ever do become a sex symbol I'll be overcoming my natural disabilities – I'm lanky, with bad eyesight. In reality I look more like an ugly girl.

Jarvis Cocker, musician and front man, from Sheffield

If people are trying to bring you down, it only means that you are above them.

Oliver Sykes, rock-metal front man, Sheffield

I know a few two-faced people but I know more multi-faced people.

Gina, waitress, from Wakefield

Those who belligerently announce that they don't worry what people think of them, usually worry the most.

Dean, naval officer, from North Yorkshire

What's more of a tragedy, that some people never realise how great they are, how loved and cherished they are. Or that some people go their whole lives without realising what a complete tw*t they are.

Robert, IT technician, from Rotherham

Someone once told me it helps to imagine everyone naked when you're feeling intimidated by a situation. Clearly, they've never found themselves confronted by three fat drunks holding pool cues.

Perry, surveyor, from Sheffield

I was a slim, fair-haired, blue-eyed boy and altogether too frail, the workmen thought, to make a cellar lad, let alone a steel maker.

Harry Brearley, inventor of stainless steel, from Sheffield

Relationships

My wife is like a mirror to me. Sometimes I like what I see, sometimes I don't, but I know it's the real me I'm seeing in her reflection.

Harold, retired steel worker, from Sheffield

If you can handle me at my worst then you deserve me at my best.

Anon, from Yorkshire (Twitter)

Any home can be a castle when the king and queen are in love.

Corrine Bailey Rae, singer, from Leeds

On those rare evenings she's not home, it's disconcerting how pointless it all feels. The little things hold no meaning anymore. Saying that, I've got the interweb thing to play with now.

Anon, from South Yorkshire

You're rarer than a can of dandelion and burdock
And those other girls are just post-mix lemonade

The Arctic Monkeys (Alex Turner), rock n roll band, from Sheffield

It's a magic feeling to click with someone you've never previously met - to develop a conversation, to bounce off each other and laugh. It's an unexpected treat that doesn't cost a penny.

Daisy, chemist, from East Yorkshire

Marriage is supposed to be a partnership. Good-looking people marry good-looking people and the others take what's left.

Alan Bennett, playwright, screenwriter, actor and author, from West Yorkshire

I once went out with a very thin woman. It just didn't work. Just this jarring of bones like two skeletons wrestling in the dark. I prefer a nice full-figured partner to tuck into.

Jarvis Cocker, musician and front man, from Sheffield

I'm strangely drawn to pessimistic men – they usually have a superior sense of humour, and are generally more interesting, more original… Then I get sick of their constant moaning and it all goes wrong.

Anon, classroom assistant, from South Yorkshire

Women are like tricks by sleight of hand,
Which, to admire, we should not understand

William Congreve, 15th/16th century playwright and poet, from West Yorkshire

Anybody who's been married to a man for forty odd years knows he's all talk.

Michael Parkinson, broadcaster and journalist, from South Yorkshire

The most dangerous creature in the world is a silent smiling Yorkshire woman.

Anon, from Yorkshire (Twitter)

Rows are so excruciatingly frustrating because they are rarely about what they seem to be about.

Charlie, chef, from Otley

Life appears to me to be too short to be spent nursing animosity or regretting wrongs.

Charlotte Bronte, novelist and poet, from West Yorkshire

Heav'n hath no Rage, like Love to Hatred turn'd, Nor Hell a Fury, like a Woman scorn'd.

William Congreve, 15th/16th century playwright and poet, from West Yorkshire

Now then Mardy Bum, I see your frown and it's like looking down the barrel of a gun.

The Arctic Monkeys (Alex Turner), rock n roll band, from Sheffield

The only time my boyfriend listens to me intently is if I'm talking to another bloke - he's suddenly all ears.

Alice, marketing officer, from Beverley

Sex is always a bit shadowy, isn't it? When it's done properly, anyway.

Jarvis Cocker, musician and front man, from Sheffield

Unfortunately men get erections, you see. And people have so little direction in their lives, if your cock points in a certain direction, then you follow it... you can't argue with a hard-on.

Jarvis Cocker, musician and front man, from Sheffield

You must plan to be spontaneous

David Hockney, artist and designer, from Bradford

You've got to ask yourself, which is easiest to obtain – forgiveness or permission?

Dave, from Leeds – trying to persuade a friend not to leave the pub

There are white lies and there are grey lies... And of course there are total bastard lies too.

Sarah, from Sheffield

There's a fine line between trust and naivety. It's easy to confuse the two.

Charlie, chef, from Otley

The only calibration that counts is how much heart people invest, how much they ignore their fears of being hurt or caught out or humiliated. And the only thing people regret is that they didn't live boldly enough, that they didn't invest enough heart, didn't love enough. Nothing else really counts at all.

Ted Hughes, writer and poet, from West Yorkshire

There's something heartwarming about an old couple still in love, living as one and appreciating every last moment together – heartwarming, and heartbreaking.

Isla, full-time mum, from North Yorkshire

Yorkshire grit

Do just once what others say you can't do, and you will never pay attention to their limitations again.

Captain James Cook, explorer, from North Yorkshire

Rome wasn't built in a day, but then again I wasn't on that particular job.

Brian Clough, football manager and player, from North Yorkshire

People don't spend enough time seriously considering and defining what they really want and why. Life is about experiences. Whatever you're striving for, ask yourself 'what experience am I looking for'? It helps clarify things and removes a lot of bullshit and timewasting from your life.

Leo, personal trainer, from Leeds

Its easy to confuse having a goal with having a purpose. Try and have both, but know the difference.

Lisa, from Pontefract (Twitter)

The mind is the limit. As long as the mind can envision the fact that you can do something, you can do it, as long as you really believe 100 percent.

David Hockney, artist and designer, from Bradford

There is very little difference between men and women in space.

Helen Sharman, first British Astronaut, from Sheffield

One never knows what each day is going to bring. The important thing is to be open and ready for it.

Henry Moore, sculptor and artist, from West Yorkshire

Don't accept that you are in crisis just because everyone says you are.

Alastair Campbell, political aide, from West Yorkshire

Use every weapon within the rules and stretch the rules to breaking point, I say.

Fred Trueman, cricketer, from South Yorkshire

If you're not doing enough to get what you want, ask yourself if it's really what you want.

Edie, optician, from Sheffield

There's nothing wrong in trying something if the only reason you tried it was to confirm that it wasn't for you.

Bryan, teacher, from Leeds

I rate enthusiasm, even above professional skill.

Sir Edward Victor, Nobel prize winning physician, from Bradford

If you embrace fear, you embrace life.

Rupert, RAF officer, from East Yorkshire

The more I do, the more frightened I get, but that is essential. Otherwise why would I go on doing it?

Dame Judi Dench, actor, from York

The man who voyages strange seas must of necessity be a little unsure of himself. It is the man with the flashy air of knowing everything, who is always with it, that we should beware of.

Sir Fred Hoyle, astronomer, from West Yorkshire

There's no buzz quite like overcoming fear. It's a very human thing to cross the line and go against everything your natural instincts are telling you.

Jenny, personal trainer, from Sheffield

The comfort bubble is always trying to contract. If you don't keep pushing at its walls forcing it to expand, it'll close in without you noticing.

Roy, from Barnsley (Twitter)

Teacher: *Don't be ashamed to look in the mirror and say, I'm great!*

Tommy: *I'm not? I'm top banana me!*

Conversation from a Sheffield secondary school

You are who you choose to be.

Ted Hughes, writer and poet, from West Yorkshire

I'll walk where my own nature would be leading:
It vexes me to choose another guide.

Emily Bronte, novelist and poet from West Yorkshire

I wouldn't say I was the best manager in the
business…but I was in the top one.

Brian Clough, football manager and player, from North Yorkshire

If you want something to look easy, work hard at it.

Vern, unemployed, from Leeds

Put all your eggs into one basket, or be mediocre
at everything.

Jamie Reeves, former coal miner and World's strongest man 1989, from Sheffield

Stubbornness is one of those unusual qualities that can be either positive or negative, depending how it's utilised and directed.

Brenda, interior designer, from Ripon

Don't wait for the right time to do something, don't let the excuses win - as a well-known sports brand often advocates, just do it.

Ho, barman, from York

Do not be afraid that your life will end someday, take care that it starts.

John Newman, singer and musician, from North Yorkshire

If you give up anything, give up excuses. We're all addicted on some level.

Tom, pharmaceutical sales rep, from South Yorkshire

The man who wants to lead the orchestra must turn his back on the crowd

Captain James Cook, explorer, from North Yorkshire

People make a big deal about categorising folk as either leaders or followers. It seems obvious to me that the best people are capable of both.

Simon, mechanic, from Thorne

There's too much talk these days, not enough doing. When I were younger there were no time for analysis.

Tommy, pensioner, from Sheffield

Proverbial stuff

Live to love
Love to live

Anon, from Elsecar (Twitter)

Gather the flowers, but spare the buds.

Andrew Marvell, 17th century metaphysical poet and politician, from East Yorkshire

Every penny counts said the monkey who peed in the sea.

Edgar, a friend's granddad, from Sheffield

The early bird may get the worm, but it's the second mouse that gets the cheese.

Jeremy Paxman, broadcaster and journalist, from Leeds

The mouse wanted the cheese, but not as much as he wanted to get out of the trap. My grandma said that. She was half Spanish, but I think she lived most her life in Rotherham… Imagine that. Don't put that last bit in.

Anon, from Sheffield

A desperate disease requires a dangerous remedy.

Guy Fawkes, from York

Don't do the right thing for the wrong reason.

Andy, decorator, from Hull

If you find a weasel, you piss in its ear.

Paddy, Engineer, from Sheffield

Butter wouldn't melt in her mouth, it would boil.

Edna, from West Yorkshire

Close your legs, open your mind.

The Beautiful South, pop band, from Hull

A ruffled mind makes a restless pillow.

Charlotte Bronte, novelist and poet, from West Yorkshire

Dreams are your mind's way of taking a dump.

Norman, social worker, from Leeds

Life is like a box of chocolates – multilayered and over with too soon.

Graffiti, in a pub toilet, Sheffield

Life is generally something that happens elsewhere.

Alan Bennett, playwright, screenwriter, actor and author, from West Yorkshire

Boredom is a luxury.

Kirsty, journalist, from West Yorkhire

Being smarter than you look is better than looking smarter than you are.

Jeremy Clarkson, broadcaster and motoring journalist, from Doncaster

Say words in your head before you don't say them out loud.

Laura, actress, from Skipton (Twitter)

Give him enough rope and he will hang himself.

Charlotte Bronte, novelist and poet, from West Yorkshire

Denial only gives a rumour more substance.

Grant, dog walker, from Keighley (Twitter)

The grass might be greener, but it still needs mowing.

Mr Chan, from Sheffield

All's not fare in love and war, you can just get away with more.

Beatrice, retired historian, from Leeds (Twitter)

Always live in the ugliest house on the street –
then you don't have to look at it.

David Hockney, artist and designer, from Bradford

I believe that in the end, the truth will conquer.

**John Wycliffe, 14th century theologian and reformist, from
North Yorkshire**

Never trust a man who wears ankle socks.

Jarvis Cocker, musician and front man, from Sheffield

The amusing and confusing…

Life is like a box of sardines and we are all looking for the key.

Alan Bennett, playwright, screenwriter, actor and author, from West Yorkshire

Aren't tears weird things? Water trickling out of the eyes - what a strange way to reveal extremes of emotion. Who came up with that?

Mario, restaurant manager, from Leeds

Do you think people with bad teeth notice people noticing their bad teeth when they talk? Just sayin' like…

Jon, from Castleford

That decision for me was almost certainly definitely wrong.

Kevin Keegan, football player and manager, from Doncaster

I live on my gut instinct...

Mel B, pop singer, from Leeds

I live my life on self-belief…

Mel B, pop singer, from Leeds

The way that I live my life is on spontaneity.

Mel B, pop singer, from Leeds

Sorry I interrupted you then… no please go on, you were saying something less interesting than me.

Sam, lecturer, from Sheffield

This place has become a vacuous prison of conformity since it changed hands. I miss the graffiti in the toilets, the soggy beer mats, that old bloke who looked like he was trying to eat his own face…

A Sheffield man talking about his local since it was taken over by a chain bar

I hope none of you fellas gets stage fright, because I'm about to unleash the beast.

An apparently well-endowed man squeezing his way in to use an already busy pub urinal in Leeds

Without making allowances for exaggeration the pub would be a much less entertaining experience.

Janet, landlady, from North Yorkshire

Now I don't know about you, but at about this time of night I like to slip a petri dish under a rabbit.

Vic Reeves, comedian, from Leeds

To maintain a commitment to our level of stupidity is quite hard.

Julian Barratt, comedian and musician, from Leeds

Davy: *"Donald, are you an explorer?"*
Donald: *"Yes, I am, on account of my coach trip to Carlisle."*
Davy: *"Donald, did you take any celery?"*
Donald: *"No, because I feared wilting might occur."*

Vic Reeves (Leeds) and Bob Mortimer (North Yorkshire) as the Stotts

*This here be a pile full of spoons for my main man Uri Geller. You take his spoons away from him, he be crying like a baby. Mother f*****g, spoon lover!*

Leigh Francis (as Michael Jackson), comedian, from Leeds

I am the god of hell fire, and I bring you...

Arthur Brown, rock singer and musician, from Whitby

Sha la la lala lalala...

Tony Christie, singer, from Sheffield

If you want someone to notice you, don't frown, don't smile, don't cry, don't laugh... fart.

Graffiti in a Doncaster public toilet

Mark my words, when a society has to resort to the lavatory for its humour, the writing is on the wall.

Alan Bennett, playwright, screenwriter, actor and author, from West Yorkshire

Within these walls the future may be being forged.
Or maybe Jez is getting trashed on cider.
But when you melt you become the shape of your
surroundings.
Your horizons become wider.
Don't they teach you no brains at that school?

Words on the side of some student flats in Sheffield – by
Jarvis Cocker

Everything comes back in fashion eventually. My
clothes and general style are so dated that I'm
hoping things will come full circle, like a runner
getting lapped in the athletics. You watch, it'll look
like my dress sense is slightly ahead for a brief
moment.

Terry, accountant, from Leeds

We started off trying to set up a small anarchist
community, but people wouldn't obey the rules.

Alan Bennett, playwright, screenwriter, actor and author,
from West Yorkshire

Joe: The thing that I hate is…

Sam: People interrupting?

Joe: No seriously I hate…

Sam: People finishing your sentences?

A conversation somewhere in Sheffield

As one veteran Russian pilot dryly told me: "We have to be very careful flying in the clouds. Around here they are full of rocks".

Alan Hinks, mountaineer, from North Allerton

Don't you find it unfair having to walk through business class to get to your seat on a plane. I like to trail a fart through as I go.

Anon, from Yorkshire

Alex: *Yorkshire Wisdom - surely that's an oxymoron!?*

Dave: *You're a f'ckin' moron.*

Conversation from a bar in Leeds

Comedy is the only true logic.

Wayne, aspiring stand-up comedian, from North Yorkshire

Fame and ambition

Ah yes, Frank Sinatra. He met me once y'know?

Brian Clough, football manager and player, North Yorkshire

I'm not Jesus, though I have the same initials.

Jarvis Cocker, musician and front man, from Sheffield

Ambition is best tempered with self-knowledge.

William Hague, politician, from Rotherham

It's usually an exposing spectacle when two big egos clash.

Jerry, media consultant, from Richmond (Twitter)

I'm still Sean that me mates went to school with, not Sean the film star, and that's the way I prefer it to be.

Sean Bean, actor, from Sheffield

Let's not get too precious about it. Actors are not heart surgeons or brain surgeons. We are just entertaining people.

Malcolm McDowell, actor, from West Yorkshire

The first page would be Drugs I Have Taken and then a list. The next page would be People I Have Slept With and then another list. Then the last page would be Famous People I Have Partied With and then another list. Because that's all people write in their autobiographies. Cut out all the bullshit and it's just a three-page pamphlet.

Ryan Jarman (on celebrity autobiographies), musician and front man, from Wakefield

Ignorance and arrogance are an unnervingly common and toxic mix.

Janet, landlady, from North Yorkshire

We grow small trying to be great.

David Hockney, artist and designer, from Bradford

He talks of San Francisco, he's from Hunter's Bar I don't quite know the distance but I'm sure that's far

The Arctic Monkeys (Alex Turner), rock n roll band, Sheffield

Successful bullsh'tters need good memories.

Fran, solicitor, from Sheffield

I don't really want it going on me tombstone that I was the person who waggled his arse at Michael Jackson.

Jarvis Cocker, musician and front man, from Sheffield

But he who dares not grasp the thorn, should never crave the rose.

Anne Bronte, novelist and poet from West Yorkshire

Did I ever tell you about the time Shane MacGowan came into our dressing room and smoked crack through an apple?

Ricky Wilson, singer and pop panel judge, West Yorkshire

They can't sensor the gleam in my eye.

Charles Laughton, actor and director, from Scarborough

Oh I don't know the answer to anything, I'm just a silly pop star.

Jarvis Cocker, musician and front man, from Sheffield

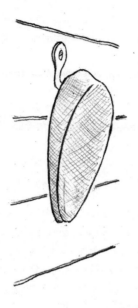

Pure Yorkshire

Ear all, see all, say nowt, Eat all, sup all, pay nowt.
And if tha does owt for nowt – do it for thissen.

Anon, from Yorkshire (Twitter)

I'm not mardy, it's just me face.

Alex Turner, musician and front man, from Sheffield

What's tha done that with? Tha knob?

A South Yorkshire plasterer assessing the work of his younger colleague

Attempt to strike up a conversation on the tube in London
and the whole carriage will look at you like you have
mental health issues. Try it on a bus or train in Yorkshire
however and you'd better be a good listener.

Shannon, from Yorkshire (Twitter)

Why would anyone question chips n gravy?

Billy, waiter, from York

We're not 'ere for an 'aircut!

Jamie, quantity surveyor, from Sheffield – on being asked if he
wanted another pint

I were lookn' for me keys for 'alf an hour. They were 'ont bastard side! Always double check ont'side I tell thee!

Matt, joiner, from South Yorkshire

Keepin' up wi' t'Joneses?! I can assure you there's no Joneses livin' on my street. I couldn't pronounce 'alf t'names! They're alreet mind.

Les, mechanic, from West Yorkshire

We talk about it for 20 minutes and then we decide I was right.

Brian Clough, football manager and player, North Yorkshire

You pay for wata'?! You must be soft int'ed.

A Yorkshire friend's Granddad expressing his opinion on bottled water
There's aifa' cow in theeya!

Kelly, from Sheffield - regarding her overly milky cup of tea

Look at him, standing there like a cheese at 4d!*

A friend's grandma from Purston.
*Cheese at 4d (four old pennies) would have been considered
expensive and therefore likely to stay on the shelf...*

She'd cut a currant in two (and save half for
tomorrow)

Same friend's grandma from Purston

Put wood int'ole lad!
(shut the door!)

Roger from Hatfield

We must be at least ten miles from a lemon.

Roger from Hatfield

I wouldn't say that I'm proud to be from Yorkshire,
but I most certainly appreciate it.

Tommy, pensioner, from Sheffield

And the rest…

(Money)

Money isn't important, but you have to have enough, so you don't have to think about it. Thinking about money is a drag.

Jarvis Cocker, musician and front man, from Sheffield

Those who say that money does not matter usually have too little or too much.

Beth, lollypop lady, from Ripon

To hell with poverty, we'll get drunk on cheap wine

Gang of Four, band, from Leeds

Money is like oxygen. We need it to survive. We make some money, we spend some, we make some, we spend some, breathing in, breathing out. Not accepting this fact is the equivalent of trying to hold your breath all the time.

Sean, call centre manager, from Wath upon Dearne (Twitter)

Have you ever met someone who was generous with their money who you didn't like? No, me neither.

Victor, pensioner, from Malton

Love is more important than money. But cuddles don't pay the mortgage.

Sophie, from North Yorkshire (Twitter)

Money can't buy you love, but it can help you find it.

Victor, pensioner, from Malton

(Politics)

A week is a long time in politics.

Harold Wilson, Prime Minister, from Huddersfield

They say that politics is all about style over substance. Unfortunately, if you take a look around, you'll find that applies in most careers.

Ali, taxi driver, from Harrogate

I've always believed that it is not possible to be in the world and not be political.

Patrick Stewart, actor, from West Yorkshire

I'm always slightly suspicious of those who talk at full volume when they know they're within earshot of strangers.

Annette, dental nurse, from Sheffield

Politics and prostitution - probably the two oldest professions. Need I say more?

Hayden, DJ, from Leeds

I'd rather someone admit to having no opinion at all, than simply take someone else's and cast it off as their own.

Sarah, from Sheffield

The concept of so-called civilised weapons of war is on par with the idea of cannibals using cutlery.

Tony, environmental consultant, from Sheffield

Familiarity with evil brings not contempt, but acceptance.

Roy Hattersley, politician, from Sheffield

There's nothing wrong with sitting on the fence if you've tried standing either side beforehand.

Graffiti, in Sheffield

I can accept a bull-shitter if he's an entertaining performer. And I can cope with a bore if he's accurate and well informed.

Tess, from Knaresborough (Twitter)

(Work)

I think you should take your job seriously but not your self – that is the best combination.

Dame Judi Dench, actor, from York

This is the only job I can do… McDonalds wouldn't employ me.

Ryan Jarman, musician and front man, from Wakefield

Take your job seriously if you must, but learn to unequivocally release yourself from it when you are not working.

Stephen, advertising consultant, from Leeds (Twitter)

It's very hard to lose your job in the civil service. I once turned up to work drunk from the night before, fell asleep at my desk and then vomited in an office bin. I'm not sure anyone even noticed.

Anon, civil servant, from Sheffield

Sometimes it feels like the only positive thing about my job is that it allows me to appreciate not being at work now and then.

Fern, sports shop manager, from Mexborough

I used to want to be an acrobatic chef, but these days I'm not so sure.

May, young teenager, from Sheffield

Those who look forward to going to work have either got a great job or a terrible home life.

Ben, from Todmorden (Twitter)

(Music)

After science, that which comes nearest to expressing the inexpressible is music.

Alex Turner, musician and front man, from Sheffield

And woven into the fabric of this harsh existence was music.

Lesley Garrett, soprano singer, from South Yorkshire

There is only one real happiness in life, and that is the happiness of creating... Music is an outburst of the soul.

Frederick Delius, 19th century composer, from Bradford

Trying to describe something musical is like dancing to architecture. It's really difficult.

Robert Palmer, singer, West Yorkshire

(Sport)

You can tell a lot about someone by the way they play football. Not how good they are, but how they hold themselves on the pitch, how hard they work, how they read the game. I don't care what anyone says, the cliché lazy ball-hogger will always be a bit of a nob off the field on some level.

Bill, dentist, from North Yorkshire

To say that these men paid their shillings to watch twenty-two hirelings kick a ball is merely to say that a violin is wood and catgut, that Hamlet is so much paper and ink.

John Boynton Priestley, writer and broadcaster, from Bradford

Right lads, stand around in likely places.

The Pre-war Thirsk cricket captain setting his field

(Travel)

Once the travel bug bites there is no known antidote, and I know that I shall be happily infected until the end of my life.

Michael Palin, comedian, actor, writer and presenter, from Sheffield

Carrying a backpack around South East Asia in a drunken haze for several months doesn't necessarily make you anymore worldly than the next person. But I'd still recommend it.

Conner, entrepreneur, from Sheffield

It takes more than a passport and a bit of cash to truly experience the world. Seeing takes more than just looking. Living takes more than just existing. It's out there for the taking if you know where to find it. Geography, time and money needn't be a boundary.

Josh, travel writer, from Leeds

And finally…

"Both the fanatical believers and the fixed attitude people are loud in their scorn of what they call "woolly minds."… [But it] is the woolly mind that combines scepticism about everything with credulity about everything. Being woolly it has no hard edges. It is easy, pliant, yet it has its own toughness. Because it bends, it does not break. … The woolly mind realizes that we live in an unimaginable gigantic, complicated, mysterious universe. To try to stuff the vast bewildering creation into a few neat pigeon-holes is absurd. We don't know enough, and to pretend we do is mere intellectual conceit. … The best we can do is keep looking out for clues, for anything that will light us a step or two in the dark."

John Boynton Priestley, writer and broadcaster, from Bradford

You'll not get any quotes from me pal, I'll tell you that for nothing.

Anon, from Yorkshire

How Yorkshire Wisdom came to be (a note from the author)...

In October 2013, much to my surprise, I had my first book published, *The Yorkshire Meaning of Liff* - a dictionary of things there should be words for. This regional gift title was inspired (and endorsed) by John Lloyd's and Douglas Adams' original cult-classic, *The Meaning of Liff*.

Several months later, with the whole thing still feeling somewhat surreal, my publishers asked if I had any ideas for a second book. After a brief fantasy about penning the next best-selling international crime thriller, it quickly became apparent that another quirky Yorkshire-based gift title was what they required. Fair enough, and still exciting.

I set to work racking my brains... Yorkshire, God's own county, industry, dramatic scenery, no nonsense, flat caps, bitter, Yorkshire pudding, chips n gravy, under-achieving football clubs, whippets... I soon had a long list of clichés... and not much else.

Eventually, I started thinking about people. It's the people that make Yorkshire so distinct. A long list of famous tykes quickly followed, and I was suitably awestruck at its quality and quantity. I then gravitated towards the idea of a famous Yorkshire quotes book. As I got to work researching my celebrity "pearls", however, I couldn't shake the feeling that something was amiss.

The world, and indeed Yorkshire, is not lacking in words of wisdom, as I confirmed during my research (I also stumbled across quite a few forgettable ones that somehow snuck through the net). History has left a trail of astute and enlightening quotes, spoken, sung or penned by those who have lived far from ordinary lives - the celebrities, the big achievers, those in the limelight. And as I collated my quotes, I was reassured by the impressive contributions made by my long list of Yorkshire legends…

So, why this nagging feeling, this sense that my idea was missing something? Then it struck me. What about the rest of us? Is it right that only a select few, an *elite* if you will, should dominate my Yorkshire-themed book? That didn't seem very "tyke-like" to me. What about the vast majority of Britain's largest county, have they got anything else to add, anything worth sharing - anything worth putting in a book? Over the next few months, with my publisher's deadline looming, I made it my mission to find out…

Quote gathering...

The majority of quotations from famous Yorkshire people were found online, in the printed press or in books. I have also included some song lyrics and a few lines I picked up from TV or radio interviews. I should probably add, that not all of the famous tykes cited in this book are necessarily my favourite people, and if any Yorkshire greats haven't made the cut, it is simply because I failed to find any quote-worthy statements from them.

The collation of advice from 'ordinary' Yorkshire people involved an entirely different approach. There was an element of experimentation involved, and a sense of venturing into the unknown. My methodology evolved overtime, through trial and error.

Living in Sheffield, I was aware that I would need to utilise my contacts throughout Yorkshire to avoid a Steel City bias. Fortunately I have friends and family in every corner of the county. I also made use of social media, in particular Twitter. I have a four-thousand-plus Yorkshire-based following from my first book (#YorkshireLiff) without whom this project wouldn't have been completed in time.

As well as picking up day-to-day lines from the

people in my life, I also asked them to keep their ears open, which extended my net considerably. Some of the words you read in this book are second or third hand, but all hail from Yorkshire.

The pub, unsurprisingly, also proved to be a rich vein! But overtime I learnt to approach people in a greater variety of situations and circumstances. Wary of limiting my range and reach, it was essential that I overcame any sense of awkwardness when talking to new people. And, to be fair, there's no easier place than Yorkshire to start chatting with so-called strangers. Eventually, I was prising quotes from an unexpectedly diverse demographic – supermarket shoppers, tea drinkers in park cafes, passengers on public transport, fans at football matches, customers in kebab shops and pretty much anyone and anywhere else you can think of!

What to do with hundreds of random quotes…

You may notice the chapter titles possess an aspect of randomness. It wasn't easy attempting to logically organize and categorize several hundred quotations about anything and everything, from such a vast demographic. Try to imagine putting together a DJ set, or recording a mix tape, from a ridiculously diverse range of songs. I hope I have managed to instil some semblance of order, however, whilst maintaining an element of charm and authenticity.

With regard to the wording of the 'ordinary people' quotes, I have occasionally neatened, edited or refined them where necessary but, to the best of my knowledge, they were all born from the minds of the individuals cited. I have kept personal details simple and relatively limited at the request of the majority of contributors.

It's fair to say that creating this book has been an enlightening experience. In all honesty I have no idea what people will make of it! From the very beginning there has been a prevailing sense of "suck it and see" (if you'll pardon the expression). If you've read this far, there's a good chance you've found something of value. I hope so - I know I have.

Finally, if you disagree with, or are offended by any of the words in this book, please remember I am merely a conduit!

Acknowledgements...

Thanks to all contributors. This is your book as much as mine. And cheers to my friends and family for not doubting me (that much) when I first came up with the idea. A big ta to everyone who bought my first book – *The Yorkshire Meaning of Liff*, without whom I wouldn't have been afforded the opportunity to write *Yorkshire Wisdom*. And finally, thanks again to John Lloyd, for having some faith in the writing of an unpublished firefighter from Sheffield.

Index of famous tykes...

Also by Joe Moorwood

THE YORKSHIRE
MEANING OF LIFF

A DICTIONARY OF THINGS
THERE SHOULD BE WORDS FOR

Inspired by John Lloyd's and Douglas Adams' cult-classic *The Meaning of Liff*, first published thirty years ago, *The Yorkshire Meaning of Liff* recycles the lesser known place names of God's own county, and twins them with all things in life there should be words for (aka *'liffs'*)…

ARKSEY *n.*
The tilt of an imaginary pint glass to ask if someone on the other side of a noisy pub wants a drink.

BLUBBERHOUSES *pl.n.*
Holding areas used for guests on The Jeremy Kyle Show.

CROOME *v.*
To lock eyes with someone inside a parked car in the process of checking out one's appearance in their window.

NORRISTHORPE *n.*
The first person in a motorway traffic jam to get out of their car and walk about sighing.

"Seriously funny… a really original piece of work."

John Lloyd

Founder of QI

#YorkshireLiff

www.greatnorthernbooks.co.uk